OLIVER TWIST

An adaptation of the Charles Dickens novel

by

ROBERT THOMAS NOLL

Dramatic Publishing
Woodstock, Illinois • England • Australia • New Zealand

IMPORTANT BILLING AND CREDIT REQUIREMENTS

All producers of the play *must* give credit to the author(s) of the play in all programs distributed in connection with performances of the play and in all instances in which the title of the play appears for purposes of advertising, publicizing or otherwise exploiting the play and/or a production. The name of the author(s) *must* also appear on a separate line, on which no other name appears, immediately following the title, and *must* appear in size of type not less than fifty percent the size of the title type. Biographical information on the author(s), if included in this book, may be used on all programs. *On all programs this notice must appear:*

"Produced by special arrangement with
THE DRAMATIC PUBLISHING COMPANY of Woodstock, Illinois"

ABOUT THE STAGING...

This adaptation can be produced with a large cast or a small one. It can be produced using sets or no sets. It has successfully been produced both ways.

If you decide to produce it with a small cast and no sets, then here are some staging suggestions:

As audience enters they view a bare stage except for two large coat racks center stage. On these racks are all the costumes and hats that the dozen or so actors will need to perform all the parts in the play.

The following is an imaginative treatment of the Dickens classic. Some tables, a few simple chairs, maybe a bench and a few hand props are brought in by the actors just before the play is to begin. That's all that is needed.

Actors play many characters as well as doorways, gates, bedposts, even London Bridge. They move in and out of their various characters via a quick change in costume piece or voice or movement. Whenever possible, actors should provide sound effects and musical backgrounds themselves. Part of the fun of watching this play is seeing actors do this. All that is asked of the audience is to supply their imagination.

The Adventures of Oliver Twist had its world premiere at Cuyahoga Community College on February 7, 1985 under the direction of Frank J. Lucas with lighting by Scott Plumer. The ensemble cast was as follows:

POLLY BURNS, BRADLEY GLENN, RACHEL GREEN, LINDA MASON, FRANK MULARO, CARL PAOLETTA, DIANA PAOLETTA, TONI PAOLETTA, KRISTEN RUDD, ERIN SCHEIDEGGER AND JIM THEODORE.

The Adventures of Oliver Twist was produced by Dallas Children's Theater, Inc. at the El Centro College Theatre, Dallas, Texas, under the direction of Robyn Flatt, on July 17, 1992 with the following cast:

Mrs. Mann. . . . . BARBARA ALKOFER
Bill Sikes. . . . . SCOTT AMES
Oliver Twist . . . . TYLER BROCKINGTON
Mr. Bumble. . . . . DOUGLASS BURKS
Monks/Ensemble. . . . . MICHAEL SKOTNIK
Rose. . . . . AUDRA HATCHETT
Ensemble. . . . . REBECCA LEAL
Noah/Ensemble. . . . . MATTHEW DAVID KING
Chairman/Giles/Magistrate/Ensemble . . . . DAVID LUGO
Sowerberry/Brownlow . . . . J.E. MASTERS
Fagin . . . . ARTIE OLAISEN
Nancy . . . . NATALIE ROSS
Ensemble. . . . . MELISSA FLORES
Constable/Jailer/Ensemble . . . . BILL CARMICHAEL
Old Sal/Bookseller/Ensemble. . . . . ISOBEL TUTOR
The Artful Dodger . . . . ASHLEY WOOD
Charlie. . . . . MARC WALLENSTEIN, RICK MERRICK

Fagin's Gang............ BRITT BROWN, CLAIR JORDAN,
ADAM LOCKHART, JILL MATELAR, RICK MERRICK,
AILEA SNELLER
Parish Orphans ... KATHERINE ADAMS, HEATHER ATKINS,
DANNY GREER, GILLETTE HUGHES,
ISLEY MORKMAN, PHILLIP SCHUEPBACH,
MATTHEW WALLENSTEIN, CHERLY WILSON

OLIVER TWIST

A Play in Two Acts

CHARACTERS

MR. BROWNLOW
OLIVER TWIST
MR. BUMBLE
MRS. MANN
BOARD CHAIRMAN
WORKHOUSE BOYS
MR. SOWERBERRY
MRS. SOWERBERRY
NOAH CLAYPOLE
ARTFUL DODGER
FAGIN
CHARLIE BATES
FAGIN'S BOYS
MR. MONKS
LONDONERS
OLD WOMAN
CONSTABLE
NANCY
BILL SIKES
GILES
ROSE
GUARDS
MAGISTRATE
JAILER

For the small cast playing many parts, below is a suggestion if you are working with twelve actors playing all the parts:

ACTOR #1 plays OLIVER TWIST
ACTOR #2 plays FAGIN / CHAIRMAN OF ORPHANAGE
ACTOR #3 plays MONKS / ENSEMBLE
ACTOR #4 plays MRS. MANN / NANCY
ACTOR #5 plays BILL SIKES / MR. BUMBLE
ACTOR #6 plays ROSE / OLD LADY /
                MRS. SOWERBERRY / ENSEMBLE
ACTOR #7 plays DODGER / ENSEMBLE
ACTOR #8 plays CHARLIE / ENSEMBLE
ACTOR #9 plays BROWNLOW / SOWERBERRY
ACTOR #10 plays NOAH / GILES/ ENSEMBLE
ACTOR #11 plays CONSTABLE / JAILER / ENSEMBLE
ACTOR #12 plays MAGISTRATE / ENSEMBLE

Members of the ENSEMBLE play LONDONERS, BOYS AT WORKHOUSE, FAGIN'S BOYS.

ACT ONE

SCENE 1

AT RISE: *Stage is very dark and dreary. Sinister music. From the shadows enters the company of actors. Each member of the company takes at least one line of the opening narration.*

NARRATION *(to audience).*

We are in rural Northern England. It is 1837.

A pregnant young woman was lying in the street—she had walked some distance, for her shoes were worn to pieces;

But where she came from, or where she was going to, nobody knew...

She was brought to the parish workhouse where she gave birth and then soon died.

Her child was named Oliver Twist. He was a pale, thin child somewhat diminutive in stature, and decidedly small in circumference.

But nature or inheritance had implanted young Oliver with a sturdy spirit to be able to survive a spare diet and absolutely no attention and no love as he was growing up.

Be this as it may, however, it was his ninth birthday; and he was keeping it in the coal-cellar, after having been beaten.

What was young Oliver's crime for such a severe punishment?

(From the shadows appears OLIVER TWIST, a small boy. Right behind him is MRS. MANN, a middle-aged, overweight woman. She is beating the boy. He's thrown into a corner.)

For atrociously presuming to be hungry.

(Company moves into darkness and exits. Lights come up on MRS. MANN. She is standing behind a gate [an actor represents this]. MR. BUMBLE, middle-aged and plump, enters quickly and quietly behind the gate.)

BUMBLE. Mrs. Mann! Mrs. Mann!

MRS. MANN *(startled)*. Goodness gracious! Is that you, Mr. Bumble, sir?

BUMBLE. Of course, Mrs. Mann, of course, woman. Open up!

MRS. MANN. My heart alive! It is you, sir. How glad I am to see you, surely.

BUMBLE. Open your gate immediately! It is locked.

MRS. MANN. Oh, sorry, sir. So very sorry. So, so sorry.
BUMBLE. Open the gate!

(MRS. MANN unlocks gate. BUMBLE pushes it open with his walking stick. He's a pompous ass.)

MRS. MANN. Lo' only think that I should have forgotten that the gate was bolted in the inside, on account of the dear children.
BUMBLE. The dear children! Do you think this respectful or proper conduct, Mrs. Mann? Do you? Do you?
MRS. MANN. No, sir. No, sir. Which, sir?
BUMBLE *(grasping his cane)*. To keep the parish officer a-waiting at your garden gate when he comes here upon parochial business connected with the parochial orphans? Are you aware, Mrs. Mann, that you are, as I may say, a parochial delegate and a stipendiary?
MRS. MANN. I'm sure, Mr. Bumble, sir, that I was only a-telling one or two of the dear little children as is fond of you, sir, that it was you a-coming.
BUMBLE *(tapping his cane)*. Well, well, Mrs. Mann. It may be as you say, it may be.
MRS. MANN. Of course it is.
BUMBLE. Lead the way, Mrs. Mann, for I come on business.
MRS. MANN *(touching his hand)*. Business, Mr. Bumble.
BUMBLE *(removing her hand from his)*. Just business today, and I have something to say.
MRS. MANN. And I'm dying to hear it, but first will you take a little drop of something? *(Takes whiskey bottle from her pocket and moves to touch his stomach.)* Will warm up your little tummy, sir.

BUMBLE. Not a drop. Not a drop.

MRS. MANN. Not a drop?

BUMBLE. Not a drop. *(Takes bottle from MRS. MANN and quickly takes a drink.)*

MRS. MANN *(slight smile)*. Not a drop, Mr. Bumble, sir.

BUMBLE. I've come for the boy—a boy with the very unusual name. Oliver Twist.

MRS. MANN. I named him myself, sir.

BUMBLE *(takes another swig of whiskey)*. How did you come up with a name like that, good woman?

MRS. MANN. I was there at his birth—when his mother—poor child—came to the orphanage. I named him after she died. I named my foundlings in alphabetical order. The last was a Swable. I named him. This was a Twist. I named him. The next one that comes along will be Unwin, the next Vilkins.

(Beat. BUMBLE takes another swig of whiskey.)

BUMBLE. You're quite a literary character, Mrs. Mann.

MRS. MANN. Quite. Quite. *(Takes a swig for herself)*

BUMBLE. A literary character; do you not comprehend the brilliance of my wit—a literary character.

MRS. MANN. Yes, ha, ha, you have quite a wit. *(Under her breath.)* You husky hog.

BUMBLE. What did you say, my sweet?

MRS. MANN. A frog. I had one in my throat. *(Hands bottle to BUMBLE who drinks.)*

BUMBLE. Oliver is too old to remain here. The board chairman wishes to see him immediately, to determine which workhouse he'll be sent to. So let me see the little bastard at once.

MRS. MANN. At once! *(Takes another swig.)* At once!

BUMBLE. Mrs. Mann.

MRS. MANN. Yes, Mr. Bumble, dear.

(BUMBLE puts out his hand to her. MRS. MANN touches it gently. He shakes his head and takes the bottle from her other hand. She moves upstage to OLIVER, disappointed. BUMBLE takes another swig.)

MRS. MANN *(to OLIVER)*. Now, come now, my dear child.

OLIVER. Are you speaking to me, Mrs. Mann?

MRS. MANN *(back to her old self)*. Get up! You ungrateful bugger. Before I... *(Sweetly.)* Now, Oliver, Mr. Bumble has come to see you. He wants to help you. So be on your best. *(Grabs his arm tightly.)* Understand?

OLIVER. Yes, Mrs. Mann.

MRS. MANN *(moves OLIVER to BUMBLE)*. Mr. Bumble, here is our little angel. Oliver, dear, this is Mr. Bumble. Make a bow to the nice gentleman. *(OLIVER bows to BUMBLE.)* Mr. Bumble is the parish beadle. He has come to take you to meet the board chairman.

OLIVER. Who is that, Mrs. Mann?

BUMBLE. You'll soon find out. *(Pompous, majestic, slightly drunk.)* Now come along, boy.

OLIVER *(to MRS. MANN)*. Must I?

MRS. MANN. You are a parish orphan. Mr. Bumble is in charge of the care of parish orphans. You do as he says.

BUMBLE. Oliver, for nine years you have lived off the generosity of the parish and the kindness of dear Mrs. Mann. It is time to repay the great burden we have all had of keeping you alive.

OLIVER. A burden, sir?

MRS. MANN. A burden. Now, hush, Oliver.

BUMBLE *(tapping his cane firmly on OLIVER's head).* Let's go, boy. Off to the board chairman.

(BUMBLE and OLIVER start to leave.)

MRS. MANN. Good day, Mr. Bumble. Come back soon.

BUMBLE. Good day, Mrs. Mann. I will. *(Whiskey is now really affecting him.)* Thank you for the refreshments.

MRS. MANN. You're most welcome, sir. *(As OLIVER and BUMBLE walk.)* Watch out for Oliver. He has a mind of his own. An occasional whipping with a thick belt or heavy stick does the trick.

BUMBLE. Don't worry your pretty blue eyes.

MRS. MANN. They're green.

BUMBLE. Don't worry, I will take care of the wretch. A boy of his age only needs the firm hand of a man. *(To OLIVER.)* This way, young man.

(BUMBLE pokes OLIVER with his cane. Music. They walk to other side of stage. MRS. MANN takes another swig and exits.)

NARRATION *(various company members take turns doing narration).*

With a slice of stale bread in his hand, and the little brown-cloth parish cap on his head, Oliver was then led away by Mr. Bumble from the wretched home where one kind word or look had never lightened the gloom of Oliver's infant years.

And yet Oliver burst into an agony of childish grief as the orphanage gate closed after him.

Wretched as were the little companions in misery he was leaving behind, they were the only friends he had known, and a sense of his loneliness in the great wide world sank into the child's heart for the first time.

Oliver had not been within the walls of the workhouse a quarter of an hour, when Mr. Bumble informed him he was ordered to meet the chairman of the board.

(BUMBLE brings OLIVER in front of stern-looking BOARD CHAIRMAN. He is wearing a white waistcoat.)

BUMBLE. Bow to the chairman.

(OLIVER brushes away his tears and does.)

CHAIRMAN. So boy, you know you have no mother or father. That you were brought up at the kindness and prayers of the parish. You know that, don't you?

OLIVER. Yes.

BUMBLE. "Sir."

OLIVER. Yes, "sir." I know all that. But, it was not my fault.

CHAIRMAN. It was.

BUMBLE *(swaying a bit—the effects of the whiskey)*. Yes, it was.

CHAIRMAN. You are a sinner. You wouldn't be growing up in an orphanage if you weren't. Do you understand that, boy?

OLIVER. No, sir.

BUMBLE. Oliver!

CHAIRMAN. Bumble!

BUMBLE. Yes, sir. Oh. *(Pokes OLIVER with his cane.)*

CHAIRMAN. Sinner, you're a sinner. Do you understand, boy?

(BUMBLE pokes OLIVER again.)

OLIVER. Yes, sir, I understand ... sir.

CHAIRMAN. Good, and since you are no longer a child ...

OLIVER. I am nine years old, sir. My birthday is today, sir.

(BUMBLE gives him a rap to be quiet.)

CHAIRMAN. You will start to repay your debt by working at the workhouse with the older boys. And if you work hard and do as you're told, Mr. Bumble here will find you someone you can apprentice with, who will teach you a craft, a trade. So you won't have to live off our generosity any longer. Understand, boy?

OLIVER. Yes, sir.

CHAIRMAN. Mr. Bumble.

BUMBLE *(swaying and falling asleep standing up)*. As ...

CHAIRMAN. Bumble, you ass!

BUMBLE *(startled)*. Yes, sir.

CHAIRMAN. Take Oliver over to the house. The older boys will take care of this wretch's obstinate behavior immediately. Make sure he is well fed—he's much too thin and pale to carry his workload.

BUMBLE. Yes, sir. Come on, wretch. (*Pokes OLIVER as they start to leave.*)
CHAIRMAN. Oliver.
OLIVER. Yes, sir?
CHAIRMAN. I will pray for you ... for your sins.

(*OLIVER is again poked by BUMBLE.*)

OLIVER. Thank you, sir.

(*OLIVER and BUMBLE move to other side of stage. BUMBLE is grabbing him around the collar. CHAIR-MAN reverently exits.*)

NARRATION.

The room in which the boys were fed was a large, damp stone hall. There each workhouse boy was given one bowl of gruel a day.

The bowls never needed washing. The boys, so hungry, would polish them with their spoons till they shone again.

(*Music. WORKHOUSE BOYS [only a few are needed] enter carrying bowls and spoons. A BOY hands OLIVER a bowl and spoon.*)

OLIVER. Thank you.

(*Another BOY enters with kettle and ladle. He hands it to BUMBLE, who pours BOYS' gruel. OLIVER is anx-*

iously waiting his turn. OLIVER gets his "food." He gets ready to start eating when BUMBLE slaps his hand.)

BUMBLE. Wait, impatient boy! We must first give thanks. *(To other BOYS.)* Let us pray. *(Sudden silence, BOYS including OLIVER have their hands folded.)* O Lord, Giver of life. We thank Thee for Thy kindness. For Thy generosity, to all these miserable creatures. Forgive them of their sins. May they find happiness in Thy mercy. We thank Thee O Lord for the food you have blessed us with today. Amen.

BOYS. Amen.

OLIVER. Amen.

(BOYS quickly down their food. OLIVER does the same.)

OLIVER. Mr. Bumble, sir.

BUMBLE. What is it?

OLIVER. Please, sir. I want some more.

BUMBLE. What! *(To BOYS, BOYS snickering.)* Silence! *(BOYS eye OLIVER.)* What did you say, Oliver?

OLIVER. Please, sir, I want some more.

BUMBLE *(incredulous)*. You want some more? My Lord, Oliver! Is that all you do—take, take, take? Don't you know the Poor Laws?

OLIVER. No, sir.

BUMBLE. The Poor Laws state that you get one bowl for supper. No more, no less.

OLIVER. I didn't know, sir. I am sorry.

BUMBLE. Sorry? Sorry? It's too late to be sorry. *(BUMBLE strikes OLIVER with his hand on the forehead.*

OLIVER falls to floor. His forehead is bleeding. BUM-BLE drags OLIVER to other side of stage.) To the dark rat-filled cellar you go. Where you'll stay all alone—with only the vermin to keep you company. And without food—oh, greedy one, or water, until... Until God gives me the strength to forgive you. You ungrateful child. You miserable good-for-nothing.

(BUMBLE throws OLIVER in dark corner. OLIVER starts to cry. Lights come up downstage on SOWER-BERRY. He is a tall, thin sinister-looking man dressed in black. BUMBLE moves to him. BUMBLE is now completely sober. Dimout on the crying OLIVER.)

BUMBLE *(putting out his hand)*. So, Mister, you are interested in the boy?

SOWERBERRY *(doesn't shake BUMBLE's hand)*. For the right price I am.

BUMBLE. The parish is willing to give you four pounds. Only four pounds for such a hard-working, intelligent lad as Oliver.

SOWERBERRY. Six pounds. That's what your notice said.

BUMBLE. Five pounds for him. Not a shilling more.

SOWERBERRY. Six pounds. Not a shilling less.

BUMBLE *(beat)*. I will bring you the boy.

SOWERBERRY. Six pounds, Mr. Bumble.

BUMBLE *(mimicking SOWERBERRY as he moves to where OLIVER is lying)*. "Six pounds, Mr. Bumble. Six pounds." *(Takes from his coat pocket a cap.)* Oliver, come here, child.

OLIVER. Please, sir. Don't beat me again!

BUMBLE. Oliver, get up!

OLIVER. Don't strike me. I beg you, please.
BUMBLE. You will apprentice for Mr. Sowerberry. The undertaker. If he accepts you. Now, come with me. *(Grabs OLIVER's hand and moves to SOWERBERRY.)* Mr. Sowerberry, here! I've brought you the boy.

(OLIVER makes a bow.)

SOWERBERRY. Oh, so this is the boy, is it? Dear me, he is very small.
BUMBLE. Why, he *is*. Rather small. He *is* small. There is no denying it. But he's strong for his size. He'll grow, Mr. Sowerberry, he'll grow. He's clever and quick with the mind.
SOWERBERRY. Oh, I dare say he will be on *my* food and drink. I see no saving in parish children, not I, for they always cost more to keep than they're worth.
BUMBLE *(looking at OLIVER, wanting to get rid of him)*. Six pounds, sir.
SOWERBERRY *(staring at OLIVER like he was a piece of meat)*. Seven.
BUMBLE. Seven it is.
SOWERBERRY. All right, Bumble, it's a deal. *(Shakes hands with BUMBLE.)*
BUMBLE. I am most grateful.

(SOWERBERRY puts out hand. BUMBLE pays him the seven pounds. BUMBLE starts to leave.)

BUMBLE. You drive a hard bargain. Good day, Mr. Sowerberry.
OLIVER. Mr. Bumble, sir. Don't leave me with him, please.

BUMBLE *(stops, looks at OLIVER and pompously walks).* Good riddance, boy. *(Exits, OLIVER gawking.)*

SOWERBERRY. Cheer up a bit now, you will have food and drink. And a bed, under the counter. You don't mind sleeping among the coffins, do you? *(Not waiting for OLIVER to answer.)* But it doesn't much matter whether you do or you don't, for you can't sleep anywhere else. Come, Oliver, to your new home. *(Grabs OLIVER's hand and they exit as the lights dimout.)*

NARRATION. On first seeing little Oliver, Mrs. Sowerberry said,

MRS. SOWERBERRY. Why, he is rather small.

SOWERBERRY. Yes, my wife, he is small. There's no denying it. But he'll grow, he'll grow.

MRS. SOWERBERRY. Ah! On our food and drink. I see no saving in orphan children, for they cost more to keep then they're worth. *(Grabbing OLIVER violently.)* Little bag o' bones, get down stairs where you belong—with the rats and the dead bodies.

NARRATION.

With that, the undertaker's wife opened a side door and pushed Oliver down a flight of stairs into a stone cell, damp and dark and cold.

The boy, used to these conditions, was still able to sleep soundly, until ...

(Hear loud knocking. This wakes up OLIVER. Knocking continues. OLIVER, half-asleep, moves toward door. He

*tries to undo the chain. NOAH CLAYPOLE, a bratty
teenager, is behind door.)*

NOAH. Open the door, will you?!
OLIVER. I will directly, sir.
NOAH. I suppose you are the new boy, ain't you?
OLIVER. Yes, sir.
NOAH. How old are you?
OLIVER. Nine, sir, as of three months ago.
NOAH. Then I'll whop you when I get in. You just wait
   and see, workhouse. Now open up this door!

(OLIVER finally gets chain unlatched. NOAH enters.)

NOAH. If that ever happens again, you'll be in need of one of
   these coffins, understand? *(Grabs OLIVER by the collar.)*
OLIVER. Yes, sir.
NOAH. You don't know who I am, I suppose, workhouse?
OLIVER. No, sir.
NOAH. I'm Noah Claypole and you're under me, work-
   house. How's your mother, boy?
OLIVER. She's dead. Don't say anything about her to me.
NOAH. What did she die of, workhouse?
OLIVER. Of a broken heart I've been told.
NOAH. A broken heart? No, no, not a woman like that.
OLIVER. That's enough.
NOAH. Yes, a woman like your mother, walkin' the streets
   I bet.
OLIVER. Don't say anything more to me about her; you'd
   better not.
NOAH. Better not! Bah, your mother was a regular whore.
OLIVER. Don't say that!

NOAH. A whore. A whore. Your mother was a whore.

(OLIVER with years of anger unleashed, grabs NOAH by the throat, shakes him, gives him a heavy blow and NOAH falls to the floor.)

NOAH *(on floor screaming)*. Help! Mr. Sowerberry, Oliver's going mad!

(SOWERBERRY rushes in.)

SOWERBERRY. What is it?

NOAH. He tried to murder me. Look at me all black and blue. *(Notices blood.)* And bleeding.

SOWERBERRY *(grabbing OLIVER)*. You, workhouse criminal. Ungrateful little beast!

OLIVER. Sir, he called my mother a—

SOWERBERRY. She was what he said and worse.

OLIVER *(tries to escape from his clutches but can't)*. It's not so. No, no, no, no!

SOWERBERRY. You despicable creature. You are going back to the workhouse. You're not worth seven pounds. You're not worth seven pence. At the workhouse, they'll know how to punish you.

(SOWERBERRY tries to grab OLIVER. OLIVER breaks loose from him. He runs. Lights change. Chase music. OLIVER runs as SOWERBERRY chases him. OLIVER hides downstage. SOWERBERRY passes and doesn't see him.)

NARRATION.

For five miles, Oliver ran. Then he hid behind the hedges fearing that he might still be pursued and over-taken. Then he sat down to rest by the side of the mile-stone, and began to think, for the first time, where he had better go and try to live.

The stone by which he was seated, bore, in large characters, an intimation that it was just seventy miles from that spot to London.

The name awakened a new train of ideas in the boy's mind. London—that great large place! Nobody—not even Mr. Bumble—could ever find him there!

(The ARTFUL DODGER, a teenager wearing a hat at a jaunty angle and a man's overcoat, comes up to OLIVER. DODGER taps OLIVER. OLIVER jumps with fright.)

DODGER. Hey, who you hiding from, the law? *(OLIVER is silent.)* The law, huh?

OLIVER. I have to run away, sir.

DODGER. Going to London?

OLIVER. Any place but here, sir. As far away as I can.

DODGER. To seek your fame and fortune, I bet?

OLIVER. Yes, sir. To seek my fame and fortune.

DODGER. Got any lodging?

OLIVER. No, sir.

DODGER. Money?

OLIVER. No, sir.

(DODGER whistles, puts his hands into his pockets, as far as the big coat sleeves would let him go.)

OLIVER. Sir, do you live in London?

DODGER. Yes, I do. I suppose you want some place to sleep tonight, don't you?

OLIVER. I do indeed.

DODGER. Don't fret your eyelids on that score. I've got to be in London tonight. I know a respectable old gentleman who lives there. He'll give you lodging for nothing and never ask for the change, that is, if any gentleman he knows introduces you. And don't he know me? Oh, no! Not in the least bit by no means. Certainly not. *(Smiles at his own playfulness.)*

OLIVER. I'm Oliver. Oliver Twist.

DODGER. Jack Hawkins. But to my intimate friends I'm known as the Artful Dodger. *(Puts out his hand. This first frightens OLIVER.)* Glad to meet you.

OLIVER *(cautiously takes DODGER's hand).* Glad to meet you, too.

DODGER. The Artful Dodger, that's me. Now, follow me to London where we'll drink till we drop.

(OLIVER gives him a look like he doesn't understand. SOWERBERRY re-enters with CONSTABLE. OLIVER tightens up.)

DODGER. The law! The Dodger knew it. *(OLIVER, frightened, nods.)* Don't worry, lad. You've got the Artful Dodger as friend. We'll just slip away with no trouble at all.

(DODGER leads OLIVER, quietly creeping around SOWERBERRY and the CONSTABLE. SOWERBERRY and the CONSTABLE give up looking and exit. DODGER starts laughing hysterically. OLIVER starts to laugh too. They put arms around each other, laughing. Lights change. Evening. They continue their walk to London.)

DODGER. You'll like the respectable old gentleman very much.

OLIVER. Sir, does he beat you?

DODGER. Oh, no.

OLIVER. Sir, does he call you names?

DODGER. Only in the most respectful way.

OLIVER. And he feeds you?

DODGER. Three good meals a day.

OLIVER. Is he Father Christmas?

DODGER *(laughs hysterically)*. You are a funny young child, you're a stitch. *(OLIVER is suddenly sad, insulted.)* Hey, cheer up. I was only having a little fun.

OLIVER *(gives him a smile)*. I know you were, Dodger.

DODGER. Well, look ahead, Oliver. Home.

OLIVER. In that beer hall. Sir, he lives in a beer hall?

DODGER. No, no, friend. He lives above the beer hall. In a hidden attic. Don't worry, there's plenty of room for all. Now, come. *(Leads OLIVER toward the beer hall. Whistles.)*

FAGIN *(in darkness)*. Who's there?

DODGER. Plummy and Slam! Is the old gentleman home?

FAGIN. Enter, Dodger.

(FAGIN, a shriveled old man dressed in a greasy flannel gown, is busy hanging up wet handkerchiefs to dry on a

rope. He has CHARLIE BATES and another BOY with him sitting at table smoking long clay pipes and drinking ale like middle-aged men.)

DODGER. Hello, Fagin.

FAGIN. Dodger, who is your guest?

DODGER. Meet my friend, Oliver Twist.

FAGIN. How do you do, Oliver. *(Puts out hand. OLIVER is frightened.)* I should be honored with your intimate acquaintance.

OLIVER. Thank you, sir.

FAGIN. And these, young gentlemen, are my boys.

BOYS. Hello, Oliver. Welcome.

OLIVER. Hello, "gentlemen."

FAGIN. Oliver, we are very glad to meet you. Ah, you're staring at the handkerchiefs, eh, my lad?

OLIVER. I've never seen so many, sir.

FAGIN. Yes. There are a good many of them, aren't there? We've just washed them and now are letting them dry. That's all. Ha, ha, ha.

CHARLIE. Yes, we like to wash handkerchiefs, ha, ha.

DODGER. We're a regular laundry—we are.

(BOYS laugh, OLIVER is puzzled.)

FAGIN. Oliver, while you're waiting for supper, would you care for a bottle of ale?

OLIVER. Ale? I don't know what that is, sir.

FAGIN. Charlie, get Oliver a bottle right away. It is our duty to instruct the child on the finer things in life. *(CHARLIE gets OLIVER a bottle of ale.)* If you'll excuse me, Oliver, dear. Dodger, I need to speak with you.

(Leads DODGER downstage.) Dodger, why did you bring this frail child to me?

DODGER. He'll be a terrific addition to our gang.

FAGIN. Tush. He doesn't look like a thief at all.

DODGER. That's just the point. He is so innocent looking no one would ever suspect him of being a thief.

FAGIN. Mm... I see. No I don't. What do you mean?

(FAGIN smiles to OLIVER and gives a wave. OLIVER smiles back and waves. He still hasn't sipped the ale.)

FAGIN. I see exactly what you tell me. *(Moves to OLIVER and puts his arm around him.)* Welcome to our little family, Oliver.

DODGER. Welcome. *(Grabs bottle of ale.)*

BOYS *(with ale in their hands)*. Welcome.

OLIVER. Then I can stay, sir?

FAGIN. For as long as you like. *(Hugs OLIVER. OLIVER is all smiles.)* Now let me show you your bed. It's right over there.

OLIVER. My bed? My own bed? *(Looks at pieces of rags as covers.)* With mattress and covers. And a pillow. Oh, thank you, sir. Thank you!

FAGIN. Only the finest arrangements for our new friends.

OLIVER *(sitting on bed. Feeling the covers and pillow)*. What do you want in return, sir?

FAGIN. In return?

OLIVER. What do I have to do for you? To repay you... for my debt?

FAGIN. Don't worry about that for now. We'll think of something, right, Dodger?

DODGER. Right. We'll rack our brains real hard.

(DODGER and FAGIN laugh.)

OLIVER. Good, because I don't want to be a burden. I want to pay my debt.

FAGIN. Ease your mind, don't worry. Tonight get a good night's rest. *(To DODGER.)* You've done it again, Dodger. No one will ever expect him to be a little criminal.

DODGER. He'll make us all very rich.

FAGIN. Very rich, indeed.

OLIVER *(by bed)*. Thank you, sir. Thank you, all.

(DODGER, FAGIN, CHARLIE and other BOY tap glasses and quietly toast one another.)

FAGIN, DODGER, CHARLIE, BOY. To our good fortunes! *(Dimout.)*

SCENE 2

AT RISE: *Early morning the next day. OLIVER is still sleeping in his bed. The BOYS are gone.*

NARRATION.

It was late the next morning—the boys were already out working the streets of London—when Oliver awoke from a sound, deep sleep.

In this drowsy state he was not thoroughly awake when he saw Fagin open some tiny trapdoor in the floor and take out a small box, which he placed carefully on the table.

Fagin's eyes glistened as he raised the lid and looked in.

FAGIN (*from the box he takes out a gold watch, sparkling jewels, gold hairpins, etc.*). Oh, my fabulous treasures... my priceless friends... my great possessions.

(*OLIVER is stirring in his bed. He sits up and notices FAGIN. FAGIN quickly closes lid of the box with a loud thud.*)

FAGIN. What's that? What do you watch me for? Why are you awake? What have you seen?

OLIVER. I wasn't able to sleep any longer, sir. (*Meekly.*) I am very sorry if I have disturbed you, sir.

FAGIN. How long have you been awake, Oliver?

OLIVER. I just woke up, sir.

FAGIN. Are you sure?

OLIVER. Upon my word, sir, I just woke up.

FAGIN. Tush, tush, my dear, I believe you. (*Abruptly resuming his old manner, puts knife down.*) Of course I know you just woke up. Did you see any of my pretty things?

OLIVER. Yes, sir.

FAGIN. They are my little property. All I have to live upon, in my old age.

DODGER (*offstage, whistling*). Plummy and Slam! Is the old gentleman home?

FAGIN. Oliver. I hear Dodger and the rest coming. Would you be so kind as to unlock the door for them?
OLIVER. Right away, sir.

(OLIVER exits. FAGIN quickly puts box in secret hiding place. CHARLIE, DODGER and the BOYS enter.)

FAGIN *(glancing at BOYS)*. How did you do so far, this morning? What have you got there, Dodger? Let me see.

(DODGER showing, but not handing pocketbooks over. FAGIN swiftly takes pocketbooks from DODGER.)

FAGIN. Ingenious workmanship, is it not, Oliver?
OLIVER. Very fine, sir.

(CHARLIE BATES laughs uproariously.)

FAGIN. And what have you got, Charlie Bates?
CHARLIE. Wipes. *(Produces four handkerchiefs.)*
FAGIN *(swiftly grabs them)*. Mmm... They're very good ones, Charlie, very.
CHARLIE. Thank you, Fagin.
FAGIN. We'll have to remove the monograms with a needle. Oliver, I'll teach you how to do that, if you'd like?
OLIVER. Oh yes, sir, I would like to learn that very much. I want so much to learn a craft so I can make it on my own.
CHARLIE. Learn a craft... *(Again uproariously laughs.)*
FAGIN. That's enough, Charlie.
CHARLIE. Sorry, sir.

FAGIN. Oliver, would you like to be able to bring me handkerchiefs as easy as Charlie Bates—
DODGER. And the Artful Dodger—
FAGIN. And Dodger. Would you like that, my dear?
OLIVER. Very much indeed, if you'll teach me, sir.
FAGIN. Oh, I'll teach you all right. Right, boys?
CHARLIE. Yes. Fagin's a great teacher.
DODGER. He's taught us everything.
BOY. He's the best.
CHARLIE (to DODGER). He's so jolly green.
DODGER. But my friends, Oliver will quickly learn, right, Oliver?
OLIVER. Yes, Dodger.

(BOYS laugh.)

FAGIN. And, Oliver, you'll start learning today. Right now. Charlie and Dodger, take Oliver with you. Teach him the finer points of your...your craft.
DODGER. Right, Fagin. Oliver, you'll have the great honor of learning from The Artful Dodger, himself.
CHARLIE. And The Legendary Charlie Bates.
OLIVER. I will finally have a skill that I can use for the rest of my life.
FAGIN (suddenly OLIVER's innocence strikes a pang of guilt in him). Like me. (Beat.)
DODGER. Well, let's go, Oliver.
CHARLIE. Your first day of work.
OLIVER. My first day of learning a craft.

NARRATION.

For many days, Oliver remained in Fagin's room cleaning handkerchiefs and practicing the fine art of pickpocketing.

Finally, Fagin gave Oliver a test. And he passed with flying colors. He had mastered the art of pickpocketing and was ready to go to work on the busy streets of London.

Under the joint guardianship of one Master Charlie Bates and his friend The Legendary Artful Dodger...

(CHARLIE, OLIVER, DODGER move downstage. Lights dimout on FAGIN and BOYS. LONDONERS, well-dressed, now pass by. DODGER puts his hands in his large pockets. CHARLIE is sauntering along with his hands in his pockets. OLIVER enters with his hands in his very small pockets.)

DODGER. The first thing you have to do, Oliver, is know the territory.
CHARLIE. And look out carefully, very carefully for any constables.

(DODGER quickly clutches OLIVER.)

OLIVER. What's the matter?
DODGER. Look over there...by the bookstall.
OLIVER. I see an old woman looking at books.

DODGER. A *rich* old woman. Look at that fine fur coat. Fur.

CHARLIE. Now, Oliver, we're going to need your help.

OLIVER. Yes, anything you want me to do?

DODGER. Oliver, go up to her. Beg for a shilling or whatever.

OLIVER. But I don't need any money. Fagin said he would take care of me.

CHARLIE. Do as Dodger says. *(To DODGER.)* Aw, he's too green.

(OLIVER moves toward bookstall. MONKS, a well-dressed man with a birthmark on his forehead, moves close to OLIVER and stares at him, then quickly exits. OLIVER just stands there trembling. DODGER quickly runs to him and prods him toward the OLD WOMAN. OLIVER moves near OLD WOMAN. She notices him and smiles at him. OLIVER smiles back, touches his head.)

OLIVER. How do you do, ma'am? *(Bluntly.)* Can you spare a crown?

OLD WOMAN. I beg your pardon?

OLIVER. Would you please give me a crown?

OLD WOMAN. Why?

OLIVER. I understand you're rich. I'm sure you have one crown to spare.

(DODGER and CHARLIE have moved behind OLD WOMAN and have picked her pocket.)

OLD WOMAN. Let me see what I have in my purse. I keep it in a very safe place.

(OLD WOMAN takes purse from her bag. CHARLIE and DODGER, by bookstall, now bump her and her purse falls to ground. DODGER grabs it. He and CHARLIE run. OLIVER seeing this, looks in shock.)

OLD WOMAN. Help! I've been robbed.

OLIVER. They've robbed you!

OLD WOMAN *(grabbing OLIVER)*. Constable, help! Help!

(CONSTABLE comes running in. OLIVER sees him and escapes from OLD WOMAN and runs. CONSTABLE now chases OLIVER around stage. Finally, from a hiding spot, DODGER grabs OLIVER and they hide from the CONSTABLE. CONSTABLE leaves.)

DODGER. Good job, Oliver. Isn't that so, Charlie?

CHARLIE. You were a good decoy for us, Oliver.

OLIVER. You used me. Dodger. Charlie. Both of you.

DODGER. There, there, friend. We didn't use you. You were just helping us take a few items from a very rich old woman who didn't need them anyways. A few coins and a purse.

(MONKS is seen in the shadows.)

CHARLIE. And wipes. *(Laughing.)*

DODGER. Fagin will be very happy with you. *(Laughing too.)*

OLIVER. But we stole. Stealing is a sin. My mother would
be ashamed of me.
DODGER. There are greater sins.

(CONSTABLE re-enters with OLD WOMAN.)

DODGER. Come on, we'd better get back to Fagin's.

*(DODGER and CHARLIE run. OLIVER doesn't move.
He's feeling sorry for the OLD WOMAN who is crying.
DODGER runs back and grabs OLIVER and they move
to FAGIN's.)*

MONKS *(under his breath).* Fagin's!

*(MONKS exits. FAGIN moves to DODGER, OLIVER
and CHARLIE.)*

FAGIN. Well, Oliver, how did you do on your first day of
work?

(OLIVER is silent.)

DODGER. He did very well, Fagin. *(Takes out coins and
purse.)*
CHARLIE. He's already a professional, ha, ha. *(Shows
FAGIN wipes.)*
FAGIN. Wonderful, just wonderful! I'm so proud of you,
boy. You should be proud of yourself.
OLIVER. I'm ashamed.
FAGIN. It will get easier the next time.

NANCY *(offstage, whistles)*. Plummy and Slam! Is the old gentleman home?

FAGIN. It's Nancy. Charlie, let her in.

(CHARLIE moves to let NANCY in.)

OLIVER. I made that old woman cry. She was very frightened.

FAGIN. She'll get over it very quickly, as soon as she is back in her large house ... with all her jewels.

(NANCY, age 19, pretty but very tired from years on the street and heavy drinking, enters with CHARLIE.)

NANCY. Hello, all.

FAGIN. Nancy, dear, I'd like you to make the acquaintance of Master Oliver Twist.

NANCY. Hello, Oliver, a pleasure to meet you.

OLIVER *(senses her motherly warmth, bows)*. A pleasure, my lady.

DODGER & CHARLIE. My lady?

CHARLIE *(laughing, mocking)*. A pleasure, my lady.

NANCY *(bowing back to OLIVER)*. A pleasure, my fine young gentleman.

CHARLIE *(mimicking)*. My young gentleman.

(CHARLIE and DODGER bow to each other.)

NANCY. All right, enough, Charlie and Dodger. Oliver, I hope they are treating you kindly?

OLIVER. Oh, yes, ma'am, they are!

NANCY. They'd better.

FAGIN. Nancy, may I please have a few words—in private.

NANCY. Excuse me, Oliver. *(Moves FAGIN downstage.)*

FAGIN. He's learning a trade from the master.

NANCY. Master my arse! He doesn't belong in this rat hole.

FAGIN. You're very wrong, Nancy. He belongs here. Here with his new family. *(Holding coins and purse.)* Now, let's get down to business, how did you do last night?

NANCY *(shows him watch).* I have here a fine gold watch. What can you give me for it, Fagin? *(FAGIN swiftly grabs it from her hand. His eyes light up.)* It's pure gold.

FAGIN *(takes a bite on it).* Not quite.

NANCY. Come on, Fagin, it's pure gold and you know it. He was quite a well-to-do old man. Very generous. What can you give me for it?

FAGIN. Let me give it some thought. *(Clutching it to his breast.)*

NANCY. Give me back the watch. *(FAGIN doesn't; she roughly grabs it back from him.)* You can give it some thought while it's in my pocket. *(OLIVER is smiling at her. She gives OLIVER a smile back.)* Fagin, he doesn't deserve to live among us. Let him go, before it's too late. Before he becomes one of us.

FAGIN. In time, maybe.

NANCY. The exact words you told me when I first came to you—after escaping from the workhouse. You called me your friend, you promised to help me. Look at me now. It's too late for me, but not for him.

(Offstage, hear pounding at door.)

BILL SIKES *(offstage)*. Fagin! Fagin!

NANCY. It's Bill!

FAGIN *(to BOY)*. Go let him in.

OLIVER *(to DODGER)*. Bill?

DODGER. Bill Sikes. He's a bad one—a house thief.

CHARLIE *(not laughing)*. And a murderer!

(BOY lets in BILL SIKES, a powerful man in his early 30s. He's strikingly handsome. NANCY goes to him.)

NANCY. You made it, Bill. I'm so glad. *(Moves to touch him.)*

BILL SIKES *(ignoring NANCY)*. I couldn't get in the house. The windows were all barred. Fagin, so this is the little urchin you've taken in.

NANCY. Bill! Please.

BILL SIKES *(moves to OLIVER)*. He's small enough. He'll do. The Brownlow house is barred, like a prison—except for one small window in the kitchen. This child will easily fit through this window. Once in, he'll open up the door and the house will be mine. Fagin, you'll be able to fence fine silver now, won't you?

FAGIN. Gladly. Easily.

OLIVER. Mr. Fagin, sir. I don't wish to go.

BILL SIKES. You have no choice, boy.

FAGIN. Oliver. It's a way to stay out of the workhouse forever. Do as Bill says.

NANCY. Bill, don't get him involved. Please.

BILL SIKES. I need him. Now, come, Oliver.

OLIVER *(to BILL SIKES)*. I don't wish to go.

BILL SIKES. Come on. *(Grabs OLIVER and starts carrying him off.)*

OLIVER. Nancy, help me! Help me, please!

(BILL SIKES puts his hand over OLIVER's mouth and they exit.)

NARRATION.

The night was bitter cold.

Bleak, dark and piecing cold, it was a night for the well-housed and fed to draw by the bright fire and thank God they were at home.

Such was the aspect of out-of-doors, when Mrs. Mann, the matron of the orphanage, sat herself down before a cheerful fire in her own little room—with Mr. Monks.

(Lights come up on the opposite side of stage on MRS. MANN and MONKS. Dimout on FAGIN, NANCY, DODGER and CHARLIE.)

MONKS. Mrs. Mann.
MRS. MANN. Mr. Monks, I am a very busy woman.
MONKS. Madame, I understand you were present when Oliver Twist's mother died? *(She is silent, he hands her a coin.)* I just want to ask you a few questions.
MRS. MANN *(holding coin).* I can spare a couple minutes.
MONKS. Since you were there at the end, did she say any last words?
MRS. MANN. It's been over nine years. Was she a relative of yours?
MONKS. She might have been my sister.

MRS. MANN. She didn't look like you at all. She did ask to see the child. She kisses his cheek. Didn't say anything else.

MONKS. You sure, Mrs. Mann?

MRS. MANN. Yes.

MONKS. Did she have a purse? A ring? A locket? Anything with identification?

MRS. MANN (*beat*). No, sir.

MONKS. Are you sure?

MRS. MANN. Yes. She was all in rags, her shoes worn, her skin pale. She was a pauper, sir. A woman of the street. She had nothing on her.

MONKS. Nothing?

MRS. MANN. Not a thing.

MONKS (*gives her another coin*). For your time.

(MONKS exits. MRS. MANN happily exits with her coins to the opposite side of stage as the lights dim.)

NARRATION.

Also that bitter cold night...

In the mud and darkness, through the gloomy lanes and over cold open waste, Bill Sikes and Oliver came within sight of the lights of a large, solitary house:

The house was dark and to all appearances, uninhabited.

Sikes and Oliver moved to a small opened window...

(A lantern is seen coming from upstage. Behind the lantern is BILL SIKES with OLIVER close behind him. They move to BROWNLOW's window.)

BILL SIKES. Oliver, this is the window that I will put you through. You'll take this lantern once you're inside. Go softly up the steps along the little hallway. Go to the kitchen and unbolt the door. We will quickly unburden them of their silver and jewels. Do you understand all that, boy?

OLIVER. I don't want to—

BILL SIKES. Silence!

OLIVER. Let me go! Don't make me steal!

BILL SIKES *(points pistol at OLIVER)*. Another word and I'll put you out of your misery, do you hear me? Now go on, up you go. And be quiet! *(BILL SIKES picks up OLIVER and raises him to the window and then through it. OLIVER is on the other side of the window. BILL SIKES hands him lantern.)* Don't try anything. I have this pistol aimed right at your head, boy. Now hurry!

(OLIVER moves toward door. Unseen by OLIVER and SIKES, GILES, a servant, enters from upstage with a small candle and pistol. OLIVER trips in the darkness.)

GILES. Who's there?

BROWNLOW *(offstage)*. Thief! Burglar!

(GILES fires at OLIVER. OLIVER falls. SIKES quickly runs off. BROWNLOW enters with candle.)

GILES. Mr. Brownlow, I shot him, sir, the scoundrel!

BROWNLOW (*moving candle toward OLIVER on floor*). Good Lord! What have you done?

GILES. What?

BROWNLOW. Look, it's nothing but a small boy. He's bleeding terribly. (*BROWNLOW and GILES rush to OLIVER's side as the lights dimout.*)

SCENE 3

SETTING: *Three Cripples pub.*

AT RISE: *DODGER and CHARLIE are arm wrestling. NANCY is drinking. She's very drunk. FAGIN is enjoying the arm wrestling match. There is betting money on the table by the BOYS. The wrestling match goes back and forth but finally DODGER wins.*

NARRATION.

The mud lay thick upon the cobble stones, and a black mist hung over the streets;

The rain fell sluggishly down, and everything felt cold and clammy to touch.

It seems just the night for Fagin and his gang to hang out drinking and gambling at the notorious and infamous Three Cripples saloon.

DODGER. Ha, ha, Charlie Bates. Proven once again that you can't win against the Dodger.

FAGIN. Nancy, Dodger won! *(Collects bets from some of the BOYS.)* Dodger, won! And so did I.

NANCY. Won what, Fagin?

FAGIN. Never mind. You make me sick when you're in such a drunken state.

NANCY. Yes, the sight of me bothers you, doesn't it? Makes you feel guilty. You, my master, who taught me the finer things in life. Thank you, good master, thank you.

FAGIN. Enough, Nancy. Go back to your beer—at least that way you're quiet.

NANCY *(takes another gulp of beer)*. What you've done to that boy, may you burn in hell forever. Forever.

DODGER. Nancy, shush. Fagin, now give me half of your winnings.

FAGIN. One, two, three, four, five, six. There. *(Hands DODGER coins.)*

DODGER. Come on, Fagin, two more.

(FAGIN pauses, DODGER quickly takes three coins from FAGIN's hand.)

FAGIN. Dodger, you took one too many. Give it back to me.

DODGER. You've taught me too well, dear kind gentleman.

FAGIN. Bah...

(BILL SIKES enters.)

NANCY *(suddenly coming to life)*. Bill! You're safe!

FAGIN. What's wrong? What has happened? The silver? The jewels?

NANCY. Where's Oliver, Bill? Where's the boy?

BILL SIKES. The little bastard was shot by a servant just before I had a chance to get in.

NANCY. Is he dead?

BILL SIKES. I don't know. I ran as soon as I heard the shot. I'm no bloody fool.

DODGER. Oliver could be alive ... then he could be dead.

NANCY. I hope and pray that he is dead—out of harm's way.

FAGIN. Quiet, girl.

NANCY. No, Fagin, I won't be quiet! I'm sick of myself and sick of all you!

BILL SIKES (slaps NANCY across the face). Came so close to all that silver.

FAGIN. If the boy's alive he'll tell all about us and our hideout.

BILL SIKES. Then I'll head back and make sure he's dead.

NANCY. No, Bill. They might be looking for your return.

BILL SIKES. Bah!

FAGIN. Nancy is right. Patience, Bill, patience. Let's get Dodger here to find out if Oliver is still alive. Do you think you can do that, Dodger?

DODGER. No problem ... easy as pie.

FAGIN. Good boy.

DODGER. I won't return until I know the whole story. (Quickly exits.)

BILL SIKES. Get me a drink, Nancy.

(NANCY moves to get him a drink.)

FAGIN. In the meantime, Charlie, go upstairs and start packing. We will have to find a new hideout just in case Oliver is so unfortunate as to still be alive.

NARRATION.

The Three Cripples was not the only place in England where alcohol was affecting people's behavior...

Mr. Bumble courting Mrs. Mann.

(Lights come up downstage on MRS. MANN and BUM-BLE in her home. Dimout on Three Cripples pub. BUM-BLE and MRS. MANN have obviously been drinking. They kiss.)

MRS. MANN. Oh, Mr. Bumble, remember I'm a woman of virtue.

BUMBLE. Remember, my dear, I am a man of virtue.

MRS. MANN. Really, Mr. Bumble.

BUMBLE *(kissing her again)*. Yes, really, Mrs. Mann. Now, continue your story about Oliver's mother...

MRS. MANN *(suddenly becoming aggressive, gives him a big hug and kiss)*. I've said enough about the little dear.

BUMBLE. No, no, no, I'm most intrigued. Now what was it that his mother gave you for safekeeping?

MRS. MANN. I've said too much already. It's the drink...

BUMBLE. As your beadle, as your superior. As your admirer... *(Kisses her.)*

MRS. MANN *(kisses him back)*. My admirer?

BUMBLE. Yes. *(Kisses her again.)*

MRS. MANN. I'll show it to you.

BUMBLE. Good.

MRS. MANN (*moves to drawer and takes out a gold locket*). She had it on her... ah, she had it hidden... (*Coyly motioning to her bosom.*)

BUMBLE (*taking gold locket and examining*). Pure gold, I tell you.

MRS. MANN. I know. As the young girl, Agnes was her name, was lying there about to meet her Maker, she recognized in me a truly virtuous and trustworthy woman... and charged me to keep it safe...

BUMBLE. And?

MRS. MANN. Give it to her child. (*Beat, feeling guilty.*) You are probably angry with me?

BUMBLE. Yes, because if I had known about the locket, I would have kept it for myself. (*Laughs.*)

MRS. MANN (*relieved, laughs too*). The boy grew so like his mother that I could never forget it when I saw his face. I hated that child.

BUMBLE. So did I. (*They embrace.*)

MRS. MANN (*quickly grabs locket from him*). I'm saving it for my old age.

BUMBLE. It can be part of your dowry.

MRS. MANN. My dowry? Are you asking me to marry you?

BUMBLE. Yes.

MRS. MANN. Really?

BUMBLE. Would I lie? (*Starts laughing.*)

MRS. MANN. You? (*Laughing.*)

BUMBLE (*laughing*). Me, never.

MRS. MANN (*laughing*). Would I steal?

BUMBLE. Oh, never. (*Laughing*).

(BUMBLE and MRS. MANN embrace passionately, the weight of the two heavy bodies plunge onto the couch, as they continue to laugh.)

MRS. MANN. Mr. Bumble! *(As lights dim on them, she shrieks with joy.)* Mr. Bumble!

SCENE 4

AT RISE: *Bright cheery morning. OLIVER is eating a muffin as he looks at a picture of a young woman across from him. ROSE BROWNLOW, a beautiful young woman, enters. OLIVER is in a wheelchair.*

NARRATION.

Meanwhile, Oliver gradually thrived and prospered living at the Brownlow home under the care of the beautiful and kind, Rose Brownlow...

ROSE. Good morning, Oliver.

OLIVER. Good morning, Rose.

ROSE. I see you are regaining your appetite.

OLIVER. This muffin is delicious. *(Eats, looking at picture.)*

ROSE. You seem fascinated with that lady in the picture.

OLIVER. What a beautiful face she has.

ROSE. Ah! You'll learn in life that painters always make ladies prettier than they are, or they wouldn't get any fee. *(Smiling.)*

OLIVER. She is so very pretty. But her eyes, they look so sad. Wherever I sit they seem to be looking at me. It's as if she wants to speak to me, but can't.

ROSE. Lord save us! Don't talk that way, child. You're still weak and nervous after your illness.

OLIVER. Who is she, Rose?

ROSE. A lady who once lived here for a short time. Let me move your chair and then you won't have to look at her. *(Moves his chair.)* There. You don't see her now.

(BROWNLOW enters.)

BROWNLOW. How's our patient doing?

ROSE. Good morning, Father. Oliver is doing very well.

OLIVER. May I have another muffin please, Rose?

ROSE. Yes you may, Oliver.

BROWNLOW. That is a most healthy sign.

OLIVER. I am very grateful, Mr. Brownlow, sir, for your kindness towards me.

BROWNLOW. You are quite a young man. Now that you are well, I can tell you...

OLIVER. Tell me what, sir?

ROSE. What is it, Father?

BROWNLOW. Doctor Osborn told me that your recovery is somewhat of a miracle. Your wounds were most severe. He said he has seen few patients who so desperately wanted to live as much as you, Oliver.

OLIVER. Well, I do, sir.

BROWNLOW. And after all you've told us about your life?

ROSE. The beatings, the starvation, those criminals?

(OLIVER has finished his muffin, eating crumbs off his plate.)

ROSE. I'll get you another one, Oliver.
OLIVER. Thank you, Rose.
BROWNLOW. Let me move you to the window. Now enjoy the morning view. I'll return shortly.

(OLIVER is contentedly looking out window. MONKS appears in front of it. He stares through the bars at OLIVER's face. OLIVER, on seeing him, screams. MONKS quickly flees.)

ROSE *(rushing in)*. What is it, Oliver?
OLIVER. That face, Rose, I saw it once before.
BROWNLOW *(entering)*. What has happened?
ROSE. Oliver's seen an intruder.
BROWNLOW. Giles, Giles!
GILES *(entering)*. Yes, sir?
BROWNLOW *(to GILES)*. Get the other servant, let's try to capture him.

(GILES hurries out. ROSE hugs OLIVER as the lights dimout on them. In darkness, hear BILL SIKES madly laughing. Lights up on SIKES, NANCY and FAGIN eating.)

BILL SIKES. All I think about is bargin' into Brownlow's home and grabbing the wretched boy and... I'll grab him by both legs. *(Breaks chicken leg in two.)* And he wouldn't say another word. *(Laughs.)*
NANCY. Bill, that's enough!

BILL SIKES. Dodger says Oliver is getting well.

FAGIN. And that Brownlow has servants with pistols protecting Oliver.

BILL SIKES. Bah!

NANCY. That's right, Bill, so don't you get near there. *(Gives him a kiss.)* Come on, forget about the boy, for your own good.

FAGIN. Oliver knows too much about us, Nanc', dear. Once he can travel, he'll bring the police to the neighborhood. He'll lead them to us. It would be my end—and Bill's.

BILL SIKES. That boy could get us all hung. *(Grabs piece of chicken and rips it apart.)*

FAGIN. Nancy, we must get ahold of Oliver soon.

NANCY. But not to kill him.

BILL SIKES. To kill him.

NANCY. Fagin.

FAGIN. Better he than I.

NANCY. Let's leave the city. We can escape.

BILL SIKES. No! I am not running away...like some wounded dog.

FAGIN. I'm too old to start over.

NANCY. Bill, don't harm the boy.

FAGIN. Hush... Nancy, my dear, Bill and I promise that we will not harm the boy if...

NANCY. If?

FAGIN. If you will bring the boy to us.

NANCY. No!

BILL SIKES. Bring him to us! You're the perfect person. Nobody would suspect a fine young woman like you visiting the poor waif.

FAGIN. Especially when you convince them that you are his sister.

NANCY. No, you will not harm him.

FAGIN. We won't. He will become our houseboy. He will be well treated. He won't have to steal again. You can raise him yourself. No, Nanc', you'd like that, wouldn't you? Wouldn't you, my dear?

NANCY. Get away from me, Fagin.

BILL SIKES. Bring him to us.

NANCY. Bill, he—

BILL SIKES. We will not harm him.

FAGIN. I promise, on my word.

BILL SIKES (*grabs NANCY*). Bring him back.

(SIKES exits in rage. NANCY looks at FAGIN. Long beat.)

NANCY. Damn you, Fagin, damn you to hell!

(NANCY exits crying. FAGIN puts on coat and moves downstage into dark street. From shadows, MONKS appears. Unknown to MONKS and FAGIN, NANCY— wiping her tears—is hiding behind them listening to their conversation.)

MONKS. Fagin.

FAGIN. Ah ... is that you?

MONKS. Yes! I have been waiting here for two hours. I have your money. Now where is the boy?

FAGIN. I don't have him right now, sir. But ... but ...

MONKS. He's at the Brownlow home, I know all about it. Sikes' burglary attempt. No boy, no money.

FAGIN. But I will have him and Oliver will be yours. By tonight. I've sent the girl to bring him back.

MONKS. Can she be trusted?

FAGIN. She can. And he will be delivered as promised.

MONKS. And then his fate will be in these hands.

(Puts hands together like he was strangling someone. FAGIN looks pained. They exit. NANCY appears from shadows, pauses, then places a straw bonnet on her head as the lights fade or the curtain falls.)

END OF ACT ONE

ACT TWO

SCENE 1

AT RISE: It is raining and thundering. BUMBLE enters carrying a lantern. A few steps behind him is MRS. MANN. Both are dressed in old and shabby garments.

NARRATION.

A torrential downpour,

A violent thunderstorm—

Mr. and Mrs. Bumble—

the newlyweds—

walking towards a scattered little colony of ruinous houses bordering the River Thames.

Somewhere in the heart of this cluster of run-down shacks is the dangerous Mr. Monk's hideout. Somewhere ...

BUMBLE. The place should be somewhere here, dear wife. (*Consulting a scrap of paper.*)
MONKS (*in shadows*). Hello there!

MRS. MANN (*petrified*). Who's there?

MONKS. Stand still, a minute. I'll be with you directly.

MRS. MANN (*to BUMBLE*). Is that the man? (*BUMBLE nods.*) Mind what I told you and be careful to say as little as you can, or you'll betray us at once.

MONKS (*opens a small door of a hut*). Come in! Don't keep me here! (*Locks the shutters.*) Now, the sooner we come to our business, the better for all. The woman knows, does she?

BUMBLE. Well...

MONKS. Your husband was right in that you were present the night Oliver's mother died?

MRS. MANN. Yes.

MONKS. The first question then is what nature was her communication?

MRS. MANN. That's the second question; the first is, what may the communication be worth?

MONKS. Who the devil can tell that without knowing of what kind it is?

MRS. MANN. Nobody better than you, I am persuaded.

MONKS. Humph! There may be money's worth to get, eh?

MRS. MANN. Perhaps there may.

MONKS. Something that was taken from her. Something that she wore. Something that—

MRS. MANN. I have heard enough already to assure me that you are the man I ought to talk to. (*BUMBLE still too frightened to speak.*) What's it worth to you?

MONKS. It may be nothing; it may be twenty pounds. Speak out, and let me know which.

MRS. MANN. Add five pounds to the sum you have named; give me five-and-twenty pounds in gold, and I'll tell you all I know. Not before.

MONKS. Five-and-twenty pounds!

MRS. MANN. I spoke as plainly as I could. It's not a large sum, either.

MONKS. Not a large sum for a paltry secret that may be nothing when it's told! What if I pay it for nothing?

MRS. MANN. You can easily take it away again. I am but a woman—alone here— and unprotected.

BUMBLE *(tremulous with fear)*. Not alone, my dear, nor unprotected either. I am here, my dear. And besides, Mr. Monks is too much a gentleman to attempt any violence on parochial persons. Besides, I have very uncommon strength when aroused!

MRS. MANN *(to BUMBLE)*. You are a fool and had better hold your tongue.

MONKS *(grimly)*. So he's your husband, eh?

MRS. MANN. He's my husband.

MONKS. I thought as much when you came in. So much the better. I have less hesitation in dealing with two people, when I find that there's only one will between them. I'm in earnest. See here! *(Thrusts his hand into a side pocket and places canvas bag with twenty-five pounds in coins on table and pushes bag over to MRS. MANN. Loud thunder.)* Now tell me about Oliver's mother. What did she have on her person? What identification? What did she have?

MRS. MANN. A locket.

MONKS. Do you still have it?

BUMBLE. Yes.

MRS. MANN. Maybe. Twenty-five more coins, kind sir. *(MONKS pauses, BUMBLE trembles.)* Twenty-five more and it's yours.

(MONKS angrily throws another bag of coins on the table. MRS. MANN throws upon the table a small bag. MONKS pounces upon the bag and with trembling hands tears open. He removes from it a gold locket.)

MRS. MANN. It has the word "Agnes" engraved on the inside. There is a blank left for the surname. Then follows the date, which is within one year before the child was born.

MONKS. And this is all?

MRS. MANN. All... *(BUMBLE draws a long breath and wipes off perspiration.)* I know nothing of the story beyond what I can guess at. *(Pause.)* And for safety sake I don't want to know anything else. But may I ask you two questions, Mr. Monks?

MONKS. You may ask but whether I answer or not is another question.

BUMBLE. Which makes three.

MRS. MANN. Is that locket what you expected to get from me?

MONKS. It is. The other question?

MRS. MANN. What do you propose to do with it? Can it be used against me?

MONKS. Never, nor against me either. See here! But don't move a step forward. *(Suddenly wheels the table aside and pulls an iron ring in the boarding throwing back a large trapdoor which opens close to BUMBLE's feet.)* Look down. *(BUMBLE and MRS. MANN do.)* Don't fear me. I could have let you down, quietly enough, when you were seated over it, if that had been my game. *(BUMBLE and MRS. MANN move toward the brink.)* Torpid water swollen by the heavy rain rushing rapidly

below. *(Takes locket and thrusts it into water.)* There!
(MONKS closes the trapdoor.) We have nothing more to
say.

BUMBLE. By all means.

MONKS. You'll keep a quiet tongue?

BUMBLE. You may depend upon us, young man.

MONKS. For your sake, I am glad to hear it. Light your
lantern! And get away from here as fast as you can.

*(BUMBLE and MRS. MANN leave. MONKS looks down
at the trapdoor and smiles. Blackout.)*

SCENE 2

AT RISE: *NANCY and GILES in front of BROWNLOW
home.*

GILES. I'm sorry, but you can't see Miss Brownlow. You
have no business here. Would you please leave or I will
call one of the guards.

NANCY. I told you it's a matter of life or death.

GILES. Everything is, Miss. Now go.

NANCY. I have to see her. Could I write a note—you
could give it to Miss Brownlow, please. It may save a
life.

GILES. All right.

NANCY. Thank you. *(Hands GILES a note.)* Give it to her
right away, please.

GILES. Yes, right away.

(Lights come up on another part of stage, in the BROWNLOW garden. GILES enters and gives note to ROSE. She quickly reads it.)

ROSE. Send her to me this instant.

GILES. Yes, miss. *(Moves to NANCY.)* Follow me. *(GILES leads NANCY to garden.)*

NANCY. Thank you for seeing me, Miss Brownlow.

ROSE. What does this letter mean?

NANCY. I am about to put my life and the lives of others in your hands. I am a girl that was part of Fagin's gang.

ROSE. You—you're Nancy, the girl Oliver has talked about?

NANCY. Yes.

ROSE. He says that you were good to him. Let me go into the house and get him.

NANCY. There isn't time. I must get back. Do you know a man named Monks?

ROSE. No, I don't.

NANCY. He is after Oliver.

ROSE. Why?

NANCY. He will torture and kill me. He is a crazy man. It is growing late, I must get back quickly.

ROSE. But what can I do? And why do you wish to return to Fagin and his companions? If you tell my father, he can send the police to protect you.

NANCY. I wish to go back. I must go back. Because there's one man there I can't leave. Not even to be saved from the life I am leading now.

ROSE. You have risked your life for Oliver. You have a heart. Let me save you.

NANCY. I must hurry. If they knew I was telling this to you, they would kill me.

ROSE. What am I to do? How do we catch this Monks? The police will find him.

NANCY. No, he's much too cunning for them. But I will help you trap Monks. Every Sunday night from eleven until the clock strikes twelve, I will wait on London Bridge for you and your father.

ROSE. We will be there. Let me give you some money.

NANCY. No, not a penny.

OLIVER (entering). Nancy. (Moves into NANCY's arms.)

NANCY. You look very well, Oliver.

(NANCY gives OLIVER a quick kiss then runs offstage. Lights come up on the Three Cripples saloon. FAGIN is in the back corner drinking by himself. NOAH CLAY-POLE enters.)

NARRATION. Meanwhile, Fagin and his gang continued hanging out in the back room of the Three Cripples ...

NOAH. Is this the Three Cripples?

FAGIN. This is the name of the house, yes. Can't you read?

NOAH. Sure I can. A gentleman I met on the road coming up from the country recommended I come here. No more jolly coffins, only the gentleman's life now.

FAGIN. What crimes are you into, boy?

NOAH. Whatever will make me rich. Noah Claypole. (While shaking hands, NOAH picks FAGIN's pocket.)

FAGIN. Fagin. A man needs to be always emptying a till, or a pocket, or a woman's purse, or a house, or a mail-pouch, or a bank, if he drinks regularly.

NOAH. Yes, my drunken friend.

FAGIN *(quickly grabs NOAH by the throat)*. Return me my
  coins, boy, or this will be your last moment on earth.
  (NOAH returns coins to him.) Messing with me. I
  wouldn't advise it. Now, why are you here?

NOAH. I have this twenty-pound note.

FAGIN. From whom?

NOAH. Mr. Sowerberry, an undertaker whom I worked for.
  Twenty pounds. That's a lot of money.

FAGIN. Not when it's in a note you can't get rid of. Number and date taken, I suppose? Payment stopped at the
  bank?

NOAH. Will you help me, old man?

FAGIN. Buy me a drink, Noah, my dear. You must be
  careful of the gallows for it is an ugly finger-post that
  points the way to an untimely death. It has stopped many
  a bold fellow's career on the broad highway. To keep on
  the easy road, and keep it at a distance, is object number
  one in our business. As I see it, young man, your tongue
  will quickly deliver you to the gallows.

NOAH *(scared to death)*. The gallows.

FAGIN. Hung like a rabbit. Unless...

NOAH. Unless?

FAGIN. You find a protector, a mentor, someone to learn
  from and work for.

NOAH. Who would that person be?

FAGIN. Me, you fool.

NOAH. It's a deal.

FAGIN. I will provide food and lodging and training. You
  are a scoundrel of great potential, my dear.

NOAH. And in exchange? What do you want from me?

FAGIN. You will do as I say—you rob and steal for me
  with the profits divided equally.

NOAH. Pooh. That is not fair.

FAGIN. Then get out of my sight. But I warn you, you will be dead very soon. Like a rabbit. *(Makes hanging dead gesture.)*

NOAH. Perhaps I'll reconsider.

FAGIN. I thought you'd come around to the smart way.

NOAH. All right.

FAGIN. Not so fast. Before I let you into my gang, I want you to show me that I will be able to depend on you.

NOAH. You can take my word for it that I'll—

FAGIN. How can I believe a thief?

NOAH. You—

FAGIN. You will go to the wells of the jail today.

NOAH. Jail?

FAGIN. Outside the jail. To watch and report to me a trial. A young gentleman named Dodger is charged with attempting to pick a pocket and they found a silver snuff-box on him. They know he's a clever lad, he'll be a lifer.

NOAH. So you want me to find out how he gets on?

FAGIN. Exactly. I can't send any of my regulars—I'm afraid they might be discovered as accomplices to Dodger. Go, Noah, and report to me what you see. Run. Prove your worth to me.

(NOAH hurries off. Lights come up on DODGER being taken in by JAILER. DODGER's fighting all the way.)

JAILER. Hold your tongue, will you?

DODGER. I don't have to. I'm an Englishman, ain't I? Where are my privileges?

JAILER. You'll get your privileges soon enough.

(Crowd enters, including NOAH. Dimout on FAGIN. MAGISTRATE enters. JAILER forces DODGER to face him.)

NARRATION. Noah Claypole found himself jostled among a crowd of people who were huddled together in a dirty frowzy room, at the upper end of which was a raised platform off from the rest, with a dock for the prisoners on the left side against the wall, a box for the witnesses in the middle, and a desk for the magistrate on the right.

DODGER. Now then, what is this here business? I shall thank the magistrate to dispose of this here little affair and not keep me any longer. You see, sir, I have an appointment with a gentleman in the city. As I'm a man of my word, and very punctual in business matters, he'll go away if I ain't there on time.

(CROWD laughs.)

JAILER. Silence!

MAGISTRATE *(to JAILER)*. Who is this impertinent scoundrel?

DODGER *(bowing)*. The Artful Dodger at your service, sir. A pleasure to meet you, but I must be going...

MAGISTRATE. Stop him! *(JAILER grabs DODGER.)* What is this?

JAILER. A pickpocket case, Your Worship.

MAGISTRATE. Has the boy ever been here before?

JAILER. He ought to have been, many times. But he is very cunning.

DODGER. Thank you. And very late... *(Tries again to leave.)*

JAILER *(grabbing DODGER)*. I know him well, Your Worship, and I feel—

DODGER. Oh! You know me, do you? Very good. That's a case of defamation of character, anyway.

(CROWD laughs)

MAGISTRATE. Silence! Now then, where are the witnesses?

DODGER. Ah! That's right, where are they? I should like to see them.

(CONSTABLE steps forward. He takes an old handkerchief from his pocket and displays it.)

MAGISTRATE. Have you anything to ask this witness, boy?

DODGER. I wouldn't abase myself by descending to holding a conversation with him.

JAILER *(to DODGER)*. Do you hear His Worship ask if you've anything to say? *(Nudges the silent DODGER with his elbow.)*

DODGER *(to JAILER)*. I beg your pardon. Did you readdress yourself to me, my man?

JAILER. I've never seen such an out and out young vagabond, Your Worship. Do you mean to say anything, you young shaver?

DODGER. No, not here, for this ain't the shop of justice. Besides which, my attorney is at breakfast this morning with the vice president of the House of Commons. But I shall have something to say elsewhere. And so will he, and so will a very numerous and respectable circle of acquaintances or I'll make them wish they'd never been born.

MAGISTRATE. There. He's fully committed. Take him away.

JAILER. Come on.

DODGER (*brushing his hat with the palm of his hand, to MAGISTRATE*). It's no use your looking frightened. I will show you some mercy—but not much of it.

MAGISTRATE. You are to be exiled from this country ... to Australia.

DODGER. You'll pay for this, my fine fellow. I wouldn't want to be in your shoes for nothing. I wouldn't go free, now, if you was to fall down on your knees and ask me. Here, carry me off to prison. Take me away. (*With last words, he suffers himself to be led off by the JAILER by the collar, threatening.*) I'll take this to Parliament!

(*DODGER is carried off. NOAH quickly runs downstage to FAGIN who is still drinking at the Three Cripples.*)

NARRATION. And soon, Noah was back at the Cripples with the news ...

NOAH. He's being deported to Australia, old man. To Australia.

FAGIN. I bet the Dodger went out fighting, now did he?

NOAH. That he did. I've heard about those prison ships. There's no telling what disease he might pick up or who might cut his throat.

FAGIN. He really showed them, didn't he?

NOAH (*not understanding FAGIN's reaction*). Yes, he showed 'em.

FAGIN (*starts crying*). He was a good boy. My best pupil.

NOAH. Don't worry, sir, you have Noah Claypole now. He'll be an even better thief than Dodger.

FAGIN *(puts his arm around NOAH)*. Just be very careful. It would be a pity to have you jailed too. *(Lights dimout.)*

SCENE 3

AT RISE: *Bill Sikes' room. BILL SIKES and FAGIN are talking and drinking. NANCY, in the shadows, is listening. Chimes of Big Ben strike eleven.*

NARRATION. There was a reason Bill Sikes chose the most dangerous part of London to live in—he felt at home there with all the other criminals.

BILL SIKES. An hour this side of midnight. *(Raises the blind to look out and then returns to his seat.)* Dark and heavy it is, too. A good night for business, this.

FAGIN. Oh! What a pity, Bill, my dear, that there's none quite ready to be done.

BILL SIKES. You're right for once. It is a pity, for I'm in the mood for a little fun. *(FAGIN sighs and shakes his head despondently.)* This damn woman who couldn't get near the boy. She is not to be trusted!

NANCY. I told you they wouldn't let me see him. They won't let anybody see him.

BILL SIKES. You failed. I don't want to hear another word from you now.

FAGIN. Easy on the girl. She did try. *(Puts his hand on SIKES' shoulder.)* I believe her.

BILL SIKES (*casting off FAGIN's hand*). I don't feel like myself when you lay that swithered old claw on my shoulder, so take it away.

FAGIN. It makes you nervous, Bill; reminds you of being nabbed, does it?

BILL SIKES. Reminds me of being nabbed by the devil. There never was another man with such a face as yours, unless it was your father—you probably came straight from the old woman without a father.

(*FAGIN offers no reply to this. He pulls SIKES by the sleeve, points his finger toward NANCY who has taken advantage of the foregoing conversation to put on her bonnet and is about to leave.*)

BILL SIKES. Hallo! Nanc', where's the gal going to at this time of night?

NANCY. Not far.

BILL SIKES. What kind of answer is that? Where are you going?

NANCY. I say, not far.

BILL SIKES. And I say where? Do you hear me?

NANCY. I don't know where.

BILL SIKES. Then I do. Nowhere. Sit down.

NANCY. I'm not well. I told you that before. I want a breath of air.

BILL SIKES. Put your head out the window if you want air.

NANCY. There's not enough there. I want it in the street.

BILL SIKES. Then you won't have it. (*He locks the door, takes the key, pulls her bonnet from her head and flings it to the floor.)* There. Now stop quietly where you are, will you?

NANCY. What do you mean, Bill?

BILL SIKES *(to FAGIN).* She's out of her senses, you know, or she daren't talk to me in that way.

NANCY. You'll drive me onto something desperate. Let me go, will you—this minute, this instant.

BILL SIKES. No.

NANCY. Tell him to let me go, Fagin. He had better. Do you hear me? *(Stamping her foot on floor.)*

BILL SIKES. Hear you! Aye! And if I hear you for half a minute longer, I'll get a grip on your throat and tear some of that screaming voice out. What has come over you, girl? What is it? *(Seizing her roughly by the arm.)*

NANCY *(trying to break loose).* Let me go. Bill, let me go.

BILL SIKES. If I don't think this gal's stark raving mad. Get up.

NANCY. Not till you let me go, not till you let me go. Never.

(SIKES looks on, watches his opportunity and suddenly pins NANCY's hand, drags her, and then slugs her with his fist. She struggles.)

NANCY. Help me, Fagin! Leave me alone, darling. Bill, leave me alone.

(SIKES slaps her across the mouth. He moves away from her to let her recover. NANCY exits into an offstage room.)

BILL SIKES. What a precious strange girl that is.

FAGIN. You may say that, Bill, you may say that.

BILL SIKES. What's gotten into her head? Why does she want to go out so badly? Come, Fagin, you know her better than me. What does it mean?

FAGIN. Obstinacy. Woman's obstinacy. I suppose, my dear.

BILL SIKES. Well, I suppose it is. I thought I had trained her, but she's as bad as ever.

FAGIN. Worse. I never knew her like this for such little reason.

BILL SIKES. Nor I. I think she's got a touch of the fever in her blood.

FAGIN. Sure enough.

BILL SIKES. I'll let her a little blood, without troubling the doctor, if she acts that way again. *(FAGIN nods his approval.)* She was hanging about me, all day and night too. Maybe it's being shut up here for so long hiding.

FAGIN. That can make a saint grow mad.

(NANCY re-enters. Her eyes are swollen and red. She sits in chair and rocks herself to and fro and starts laughing.)

BILL SIKES. Now she's on the other tack?

FAGIN. I'm leaving this nest before I do go mad. Would you come light me down the stairs.

BILL SIKES *(filling his pipe).* Nancy. Light him down. It's a pity he should break his neck and disappoint the sight-seers. Show him a light.

(NANCY follows FAGIN with candle or lantern. FAGIN lays fingers on his lips and whispers.)

FAGIN. What is it, Nanc', dear?

NANCY. What do you mean?

FAGIN. The reason for all this. You are not crazed, my little actress. He is such a brute, a beast, why don't you leave him once and for all?

NANCY. I can't.

FAGIN. It doesn't matter just now. We'll talk about this again. You have a friend in me, Nancy, a staunch friend. I have the means at hand, quiet and close. If you want revenge on those that treat you like a dog—worse than a dog—come to me. He humors himself at your expense. I say, come to me. He is the mere hound of a day, but you know me of old, Nanc'.

NANCY. I know you well. Good night. (*Shrinks back, as FAGIN offers to lay his hands on hers.*)

FAGIN. Good night.

(*NANCY nods and closes the door between them. FAGIN moves out and starts walking. He hides. NOAH CLAY-POLE joins him. NANCY moves back to her room. BILL SIKES is now sound asleep. NANCY looks around, sees no one, hurries off.*)

NOAH. She's up to no good, sir. Let me follow her.

FAGIN. No...leave her be.

NOAH. But she could be turning on us.

FAGIN. Not this girl.

NOAH. You can't trust a thief, remember?

FAGIN. All right, Noah. Follow her! (*FAGIN looks very worried.*)

NARRATION. It is a foggy night. The church clock chimes three-quarters past eleven, as two figures emerge on the London Bridge.

(ROSE and BROWNLOW emerge on London Bridge. ROSE is restless. BROWNLOW leans against railing. Chimes of Big Ben strike midnight. NANCY runs in. Behind her is NOAH.)

NANCY. Not here. I am afraid to speak to you here. Come away ... out of the public road. This way.

BROWNLOW. This is far enough. Why must we speak in this dark and dismal hole?

NANCY. I told the dear lady that I am afraid to speak any place but here in the darkness. I don't know why it is but I have such fear and dread upon me tonight.

BROWNLOW. A fear of what?

NANCY. Horrible thoughts of death.

BROWNLOW. Imagination, my child.

NANCY. These thoughts were real.

BROWNLOW. They will pass. You were not here last Sunday night?

NANCY. I couldn't come. I was kept by force.

ROSE. By whom?

NANCY. Bill—the man I told you about, young lady.

BROWNLOW. You weren't suspected, I hope?

NANCY. No. But it's not easy for me to leave him unless he knows why.

BROWNLOW. Now about this fellow Mr. Monks? Put him into my hands and let me deal with him.

NANCY. Follow me to his hideout. It is by the river.

(NANCY leads BROWNLOW and ROSE to another part of stage, to MONKS' shack. BROWNLOW knocks, then barges door open, taking out his pistol.)

NANCY. He's gone. But he'll return.

BROWNLOW. I will arrange for a few of my guards to wait for him here. Monks will not be a danger to Oliver much longer.

ROSE. Thanks to you, Nancy.

NANCY. You must do me a favor.

BROWNLOW. Yes, what do you wish? Anything, my brave young woman?

NANCY. After you have Monks...let Fagin and Bill Sikes be.

BROWNLOW. But they are criminals and the police will—

NANCY. You are a wealthy man. You can keep the police off their tails.

BROWNLOW. But—

ROSE. Look what she's done, Father.

BROWNLOW. Very well. Nothing will be reported.

NANCY. Thank you, sir. I must hurry back.

(NANCY leaves. NOAH pops his head out from where he was hiding. He smiles. ROSE and BROWNLOW exit. NOAH moves down to FAGIN sitting at a table in the Three Cripples.)

NOAH. Fagin!

FAGIN. What is it?

NOAH. Nancy has betrayed us, sir. She met with a gentleman and a lady at London Bridge. Real quality folks.

She mentioned you and Bill to them. She took them to Monks' shack.

FAGIN. Was he captured?

NOAH. He wasn't there, but the next time he comes back he'll be nabbed for sure.

FAGIN. What did she say about Bill and me?

(BILL SIKES enters and listens. He looks like he has just awakened.)

NOAH. This man and woman seem to know all about you both.

BILL SIKES. Noah, what are you talking about? Have you seen Nancy, Fagin?

FAGIN. No, I haven't seen her.

BILL SIKES *(grabs NOAH)*. But you have, haven't you, boy? What about this man and woman? *(Puts knife to his throat.)* The truth or I'll kill you. What about Nancy?

NOAH. She has betrayed us, sir, at London Bridge.

BILL SIKES. Is it the truth?

NOAH. Yes, sir.

BILL SIKES. I'll kill her! I'll destroy her!

FAGIN *(tries to grab him)*. Wait, Bill, just a word.

BILL SIKES. Let me out. Don't speak to me, Fagin.

FAGIN. She has betrayed Monks, not us. Isn't that right, Noah? *(Beat.)* What specifically did Nancy say about Bill? What?

NOAH *(evil)*. That he's a villain who she will soon escape from.

BILL SIKES. There, Fagin. There's your proof.

FAGIN. I don't believe you, boy. Liar. *(Moves toward the angry SIKES.)* Bill, wait.

(BILL SIKES throws FAGIN to ground and darts out furiously.)

NOAH. An informer should be punished. It's self-preservation, right, Fagin?

(FAGIN quickly runs out. Lights come up on NANCY in bed sleeping. BILL SIKES enters room and moves to her.)

BILL SIKES. Wake up, wake up, you devil! *(Rouses her from her sleep. NANCY raises herself with a hurried and startled look.)* Get up.
NANCY. Oh, Bill, good morning.
BILL SIKES. It isn't morning! Get up!

(There is a candleholder near her. SIKES grabs it and hurls it against the wall. NANCY moves to pick it up.)

BILL SIKES. Let it be. *(Thrusting his hand before her.)* Stay right there.
NANCY. Bill. Why do you look at me like that?
BILL SIKES. You know why. *(Sits down regarding her for a few seconds, then begins to breathe heavily. He grasps her head and throat, dragging her into the middle of the room.)*
NANCY. No, I don't. What's come over you? Please tell me. What's wrong? Bill! Bill! what have I done?
BILL SIKES *(puts his hand upon her mouth)*. You know, you She Devil! You were watched tonight, every word you said was heard.

NANCY (*fights and gets his hand from her mouth*). Then spare my life for the love of Heaven, as I spared yours. (*Clings to SIKES.*) The gentleman and that dear lady, told me tonight that they will help you. You wont' have to face kidnapping charges. Oh, darling, you and Fagin will be free men again. You can forget about this life of crime. We can both leave this dreadful hole. We can start a new life. I feel it now—but we must have time, a little, little time.

(*BILL SIKES strangles NANCY to death. He then staggers backwards. He screams with great remorse. Panicking, he hurries out. Lights come up at the Three Cripples pub where MONKS is drinking. SIKES enters and moves to him.*)

BILL SIKES. Monks, I need money—quickly.
MONKS. I am not a bank, Mr. Sikes.

(*SIKES moves into MONKS' pocket and takes out wallet and coins. He goes through it quickly.*)

MONKS. I don't carry much money on me, sir.
BILL SIKES. I'll kill you.
MONKS. That won't solve your problem, Sikes.
BILL SIKES. Help me get the money.
MONKS. Did you ask Fagin?
BILL SIKES. He doesn't have the amount I need. I have to leave the country.
MONKS. Would five hundred pounds do?
BILL SIKES. You had better not be making a fool of me, now.

MONKS. Oh, no. I will give you five hundred pounds if you bring Oliver Twist to me.

BILL SIKES. Then I will do it right away! Get me the five hundred pounds tonight.

MONKS *(writes a note)*. Bring me the boy to this address. Alive or dead. I will be waiting.

BILL SIKES. All right.

MONKS. Do not fail me, Mr. Sikes.

BILL SIKES. I won't.

(Quickly leaves. Lights come back up on NANCY lying dead. FAGIN enters, sees her and moves to her.)

FAGIN. Oh, dear Nancy, it was my fault.

NOAH *(entering)*. Fagin, we'd better get out of here. Come on, before the police come. Fagin. Come on! Fagin!

FAGIN *(in great sorrow)*. Leave me be. I'm too old to run anymore. Too old.

NOAH. Hurry up, Fagin.

(FAGIN pauses, kisses NANCY. Blackout.)

SCENE 4

AT RISE: *Dance music. Evening. BROWNLOW's garden. ROSE and BROWNLOW dancing. GUARDS are all around. OLIVER is watching the dancing and enjoying it. Number ends. ROSE moves to OLIVER.*

ROSE. Enjoying yourself, Oliver?

OLIVER. Very much, Rose.

ROSE. Come on, be my partner.
OLIVER. I don't know how to dance.
ROSE. Come on, I'll teach you.
OLIVER. Oh, no. I wouldn't want to trouble you.
BROWNLOW. Oliver, a gentleman should not turn down a
    young lady.

*(OLIVER takes ROSE's hand. ROSE teaches OLIVER
how to dance. He catches on quickly. He's all smiles. As
this is happening, BILL SIKES sneaks past GUARDS.
SIKES quickly pushes ROSE away and tries to grab
OLIVER.)*

OLIVER. Mr. Sikes!

*(OLIVER runs. SIKES chases him. GUARDS move to
grab SIKES. SIKES grabs OLIVER. GUARDS point guns
at SIKES.)*

BILL SIKES *(gun to OLIVER's head)*. Shoot and the boy
    is dead.
OLIVER. Please, Mr. Sikes!
BROWNLOW. Don't harm the boy!
ROSE. Let Oliver go! I beg you.
BILL SIKES. We're going to leave your little party. No
    one had better follow us.

*(SIKES is starting to lead OLIVER off when GILES ap-
pears from the side and shoots SIKES dead.)*

ROSE. Oh, Oliver!

(ROSE and BROWNLOW hug OLIVER.)

ROSE. You are safe. No one will harm you now.
BROWNLOW *(to himself)*. We must find Monks.

(From shadows, MONKS enters. GUARDS grab him from behind.)

MONKS. Let me go! You have no right.
BROWNLOW. They have their orders.

(GUARDS lead MONKS offstage. Lights come up on FAGIN in his hideout with his precious jewel box in hand.)

FAGIN. You're all I have left.
CHARLIE *(entering)*. Fagin! Quick, we have to leave. I've heard the constables talking. They're looking for you. They think you murdered Nancy. The boys and I have found another hideaway. Come on. The constables will be here soon. Hurry!
FAGIN *(in his own world)*. Go on, Charlie. Let me be.
CHARLIE. Fagin, I can't just let you stay here—they'll see all these stolen goods.
FAGIN. Go, Charlie. Leave!
CHARLIE *(starts taking down handkerchiefs and picks up some of the jewels)*. We have to get rid of the evidence.
FAGIN. Leave, boy! LEAVE!
CHARLIE. All right, sir. You've gone mad, old man. If you're going to stay and let them get you—give me the jewel box.
FAGIN. Get out!

(CHARLIE runs out. FAGIN carefully puts his jewelry box in the secret hiding place. Lights dimout on the tired old man.)

SCENE 5

AT RISE: *BROWNLOW home. BROWNLOW is pacing. GUARDS bring in MONKS.*

MONKS. By what authority am I kidnapped in the street and brought here by these dogs?

BROWNLOW. By mine. *(To GUARDS.)* That will be all.

(GUARDS leave.)

MONKS. I am leaving. *(Starts to walk out.)*

BROWNLOW. Wait right there, Mr. Edward Leeford.

MONKS. Monks is my name, sir.

BROWNLOW. Edward Leeford. I was your father Philip's best friend.

MONKS. This is petty treatment from my father's best friend.

BROWNLOW. It is because I was your father's best friend that I have brought you here rather than to a jail.

MONKS. On what charges?

BROWNLOW. You know, your father's marriage was an unhappy one. And when he left your mother he moved into the country. There he met a lovely young girl and they became lovers.

MONKS. I have heard these stories.

BROWNLOW. Her name was Agnes Fleming. He kept his marriage a secret from her. Even when he returned to London to ask your mother for a divorce, he still didn't tell Agnes anything.

MONKS. I can see what you're leading to. I suppose that Agnes became pregnant.

BROWNLOW. Before your father went on business in Paris, he visited me in this very room. Among the things he left me was a portrait of this poor girl. He also left me his will.

MONKS. A will?

BROWNLOW. He told me he had a premonition that he would die abroad. In the will, he left something for your mother with the rest going to Agnes Fleming.

MONKS. And she received the rest of the money?

BROWNLOW. No, I was never able to find her. You received all his money when your mother died. Agnes believed that she was abandoned by your father. She ran away, never to be heard from again...until we saw Oliver.

MONKS. It is an interesting story, now if you'll excuse me.

BROWNLOW. Wait! (*Exits stage, then quickly returns with OLIVER.*) This, Edward, is the innocent you've been trying to have murdered.

MONKS. I think you are a very sick man. I would not harm this child.

BROWNLOW. Oliver, is this the man?

OLIVER. Yes.

MONKS. What is it, boy?

BROWNLOW. Oliver has seen you twice staring at him.

MONKS. Since when is gazing at someone a crime?

BROWNLOW. But trying to have him murdered is.

MONKS. One more accusation that my attorney can use in court.

BROWNLOW. Nancy, the murdered girl, overheard you and Fagin plotting the murder of this child. It was so Oliver would not get his half of the inheritance, am I right, Edward?

MONKS. Huh. What kind of proof is that? From a dead whore, a lying criminal.

OLIVER. She wasn't that at all. She wasn't!

BROWNLOW *(hugging OLIVER)*. She wasn't that at all. You can go, Oliver.

(OLIVER and MONKS exchange stares as OLIVER exits.)

MONKS. Sir, I am *now* also leaving. You have wasted my time and caused me much abuse. Besides, you have found no proof at all that the boy is my half-brother.

BROWNLOW. But I bet you have.

MONKS *(beat)*. There is no point to this conversation. Goodbye. *(Exits.)*

BROWNLOW. Fagin!

(Lights come up on FAGIN rocking in his prison stone seat back and forth.)

FAGIN. Good boy, Charlie, well done. Oliver, too, ha, ha, ha. Oliver too—quite the gentleman now—quite the— take that boy away to bed.

(OLIVER and BROWNLOW enter with JAILER.)

JAILER. Now don't be alarmed, boy, the old man has lost
   his mind.

FAGIN. Take him away to bed. Do you hear me, some of
   you? He has been— somehow—the cause of all this. It's
   worth the money to bring him up to it. Bill, never mind
   the girl. Leave the girl alone! Bill!

JAILER. Bill!

FAGIN. That's me. An old man, my lord, waiting to face
   the hangman tomorrow. A very old, old man. *(Notices
   OLIVER and BROWNLOW.)* What do you want of me?
   What?

JAILER. Steady. Now, sir, tell him what you want? Quick,
   if you please, for he grows worse as the time gets on.

BROWNLOW. Did a Mr. Monks tell you about a locket, or
   a ring or some papers that shows who Oliver's mother
   was. An object that he destroyed.

FAGIN. No, I haven't heard of any papers, or rings or
   lockets.

BROWNLOW. For the love of God, are you sure? Please
   try to remember if Monks ever mentioned some object
   that belonged to Oliver's mother.

FAGIN. Oliver. Here, here. Let me whisper to you.

*(OLIVER relinquishes BROWNLOW's hand and moves
alone to FAGIN.)*

FAGIN. Oliver, dear. Monks once told me—during one of
   our drunken moods—that he received a locket from
   Bumble. It has "Agnes" engraved in it. I want to talk to
   you, my dear. I want to talk to you.

OLIVER. Yes, yes?

FAGIN. Outside, outside. Say I've gone to sleep—they'll believe you. You can get me out, if you take me so. Now then, now then.

OLIVER. Oh. God forgive this poor man. *(Bursts into tears.)*

FAGIN. That's right, that's right. They'll help us on. This door first. If I shake and tremble, as we pass the gallows, don't you mind, but hurry on. Now. Now. Now.

JAILER. Have you nothing else to ask him, sir?

BROWNLOW. Is there any proof of Oliver's proper birth?

FAGIN. Well, well. There was a locket that Monks had told me about...he had received it from a Mrs. Bumble. He threw it into the River Thames.

BROWNLOW. Thank you, Fagin. We must leave now, Oliver.

OLIVER. Yes, sir.

FAGIN. I loved her, Oliver. I loved Nancy. She was like a daughter.

(Door to cell locks and slams shut as OLIVER and BROWNLOW exit. BROWNLOW has his arm around OLIVER. OLIVER exits. Lights come up on MAGISTRATE and ROSE. OLIVER and BROWNLOW move to them.)

ROSE. Father, they have arrived.

BROWNLOW. Good. Tell, Giles to let them in.

(ROSE moves offstage and motions to GILES.)

BROWNLOW. Magistrate, pay close attention, please.

BUMBLE *(entering)*. Do my eyes deceive me or is that little Oliver? Oh, O-l-i-v-e-r! If you only knew how I missed you.

MRS. MANN *(entering)*. Hold your tongue, fool.

OLIVER. Mrs. Mann.

MRS. MANN *(disliking it)*. Mrs. Bumble.

BUMBLE. Oliver, dear, you wouldn't believe how much I've worried.

MRS. MANN. Hold your tongue, I say!

BUMBLE. Isn't nature, nature, Mrs. Bumble. Can't I be supposed to feel— I as brought him up parochially— when I see him a-setting here among ladies and gentlemen of the most affable description.

BROWNLOW. Do you know a Mr. Monks?

BUMBLE. Yes.

MRS. MANN. No.

BUMBLE. No.

BROWNLOW. So you do, Mr. Bumble?

BUMBLE. Perhaps I've heard the name.

BROWNLOW. Have you ever sold him anything?

MRS. MANN. No.

BROWNLOW. A certain gold locket?

BUMBLE. Well...

MRS. MANN. Certainly not. Why are we brought here to answer to such nonsense as this?

BROWNLOW. We know that you had the locket and that you sold it to a Mr. Monks, who threw it in the river.

MRS. MANN. No, you have the wrong party.

BUMBLE. Yes, definitely the wrong party.

BROWNLOW. A locket read Agnes Fleming on it.

BUMBLE. Only Agnes, the rest was blank. Oh!

MRS. MANN. You ninny!

BROWNLOW. Enough proof, Magistrate?

MAGISTRATE. Enough.

BUMBLE. Magistrate? I hope, kind sir, that this unfortunate little circumstance will not deprive me of my parochial office?

MAGISTRATE. Indeed it will. You may make up your mind to that, and think yourself lucky that we don't press charges against you.

BUMBLE. It was all Mrs. Bumble here.

MAGISTRATE. That is no excuse. You were present on the occasion of the destruction of the trinket, and indeed are the most guilty of the two, in the eye of the law. For the law supposes that your wife acts under your direction.

BUMBLE. If the law supposes that, the law is an ass—an idiot. If that's the eye of the law, the law is a bachelor. *(Fixes his hat on very tight, puts his hands in his pocket and starts to leave. MRS. MANN, very angry, follows.)*

ROSE. He's a terrible liar.

BROWNLOW. He should be jailed as his punishment.

MAGISTRATE. Why use taxpayers' money when he will have the wrath of that woman to contend with for the rest of his life.

ROSE. Oliver, we now have proof that that picture was your mother.

BROWNLOW. You have a home with us forever.

(OLIVER hugs ROSE and BROWNLOW.)

THE END

DIRECTOR'S NOTES

DIRECTOR'S NOTES

DIRECTOR'S NOTES